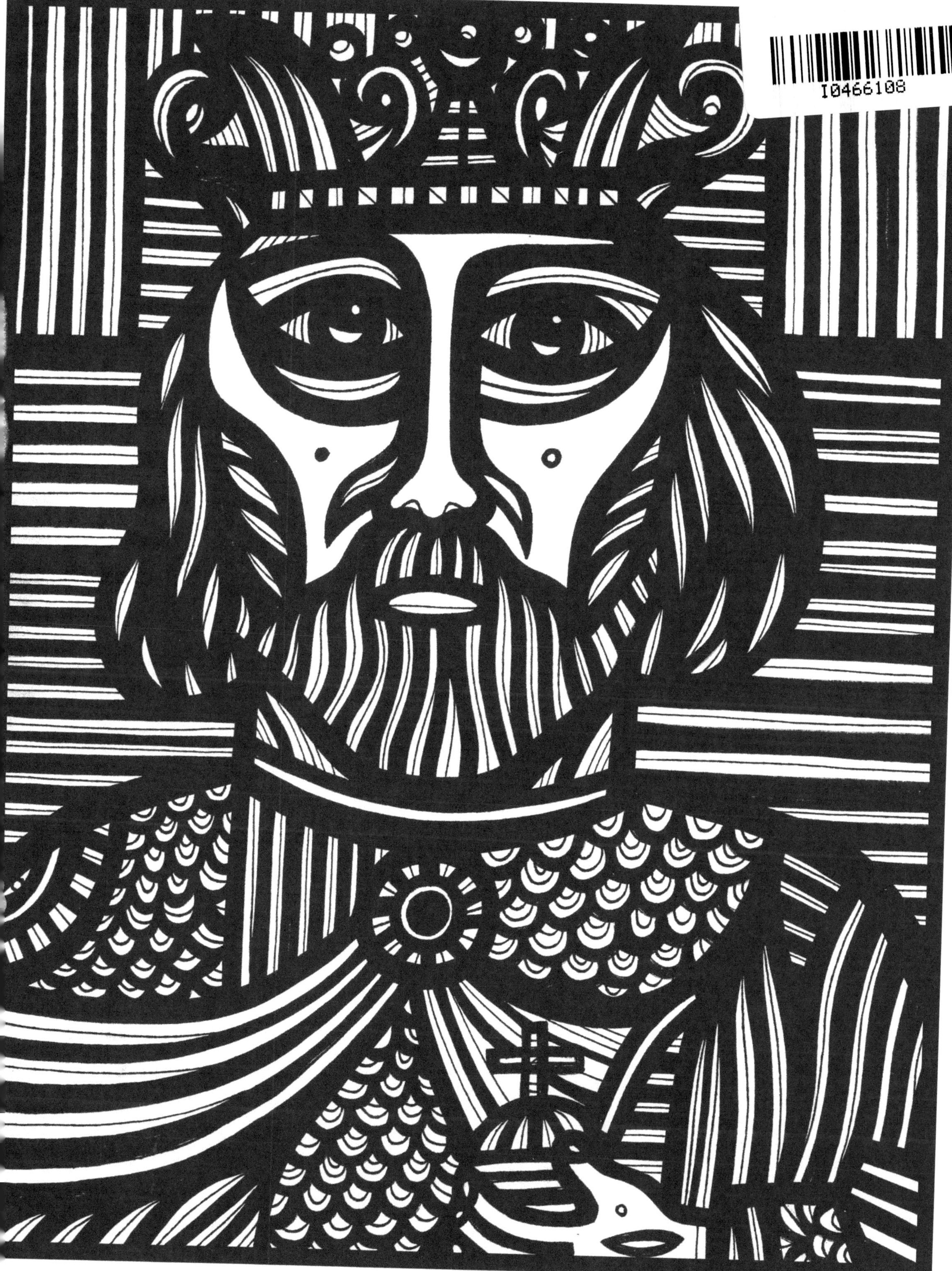

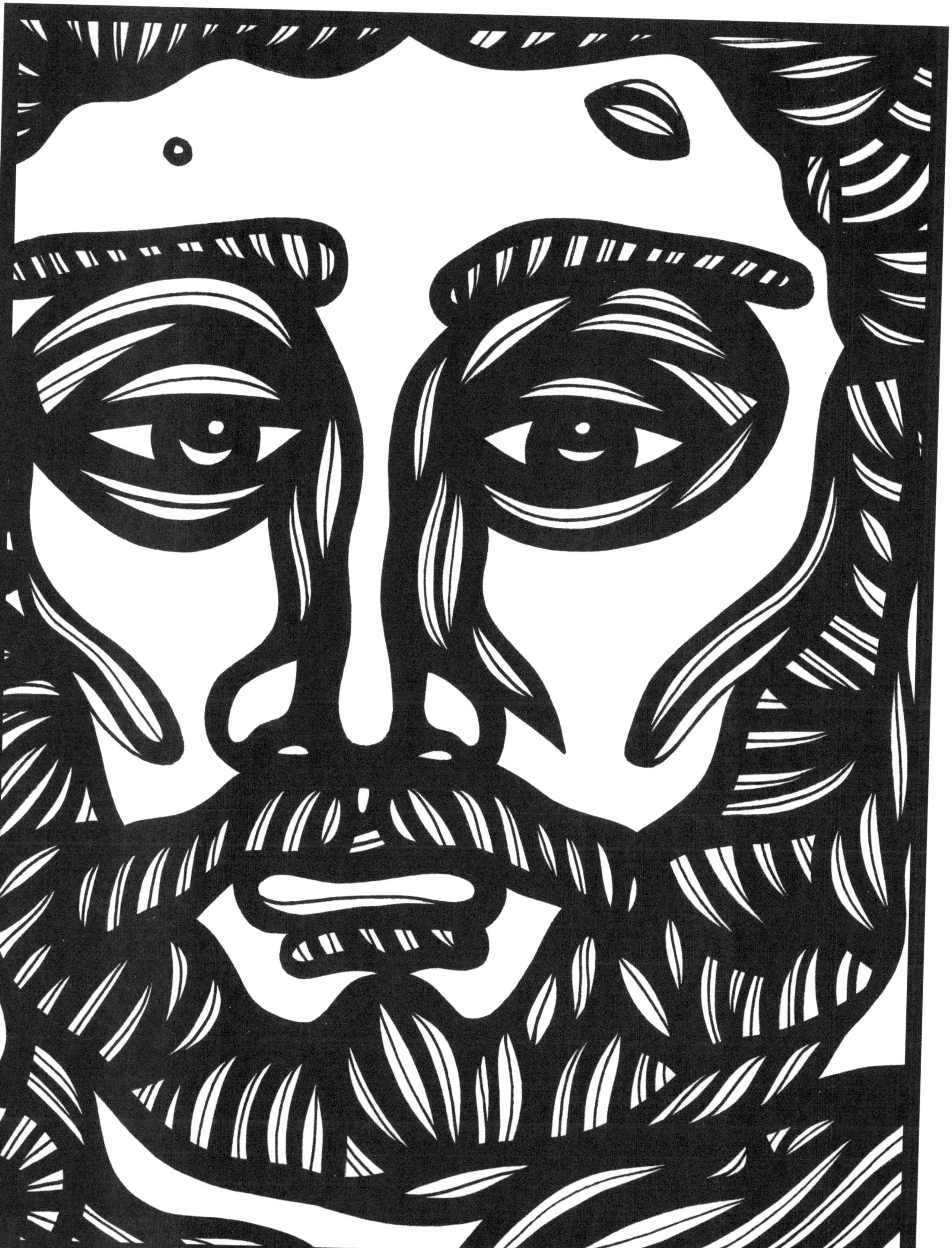

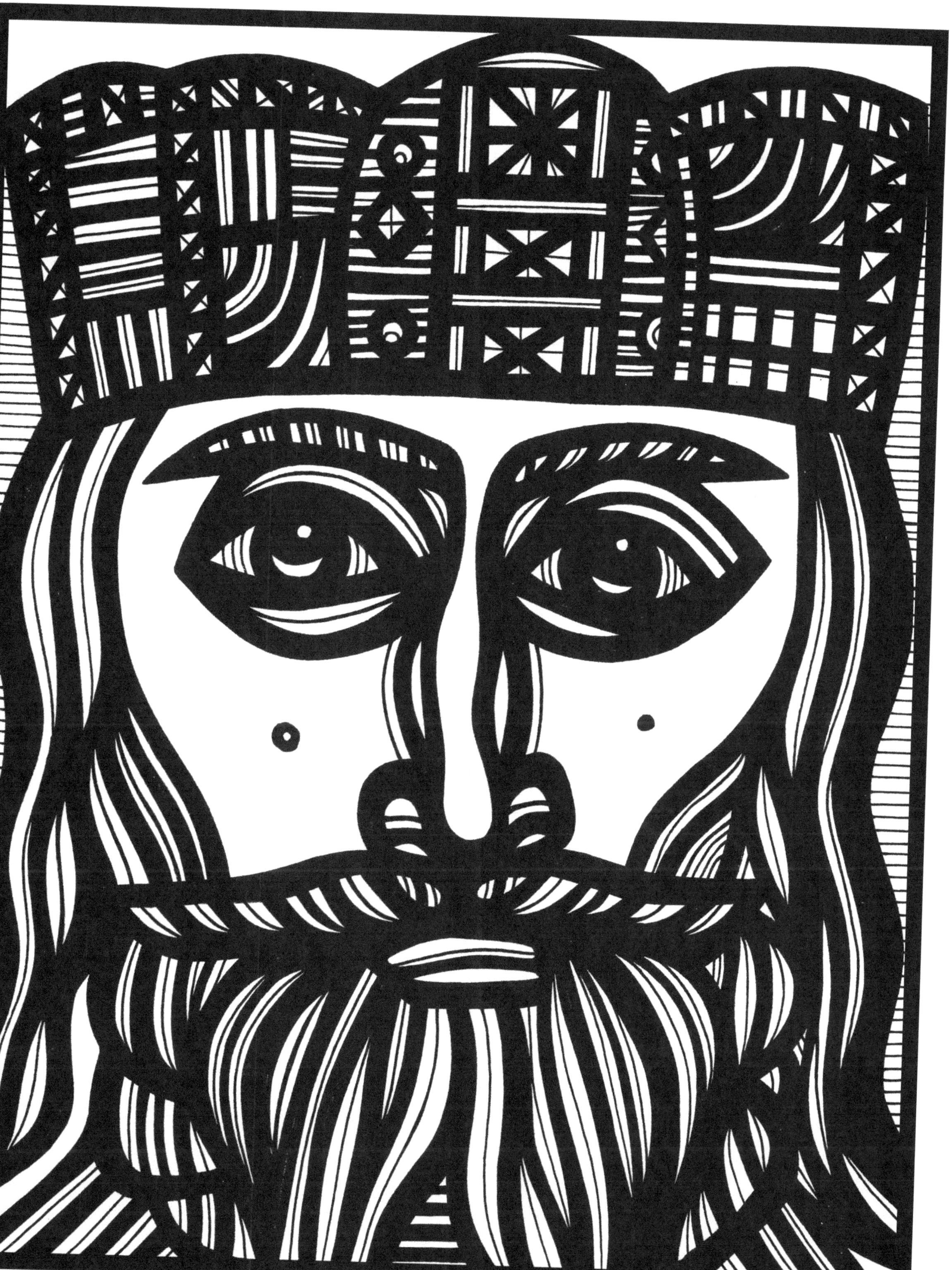

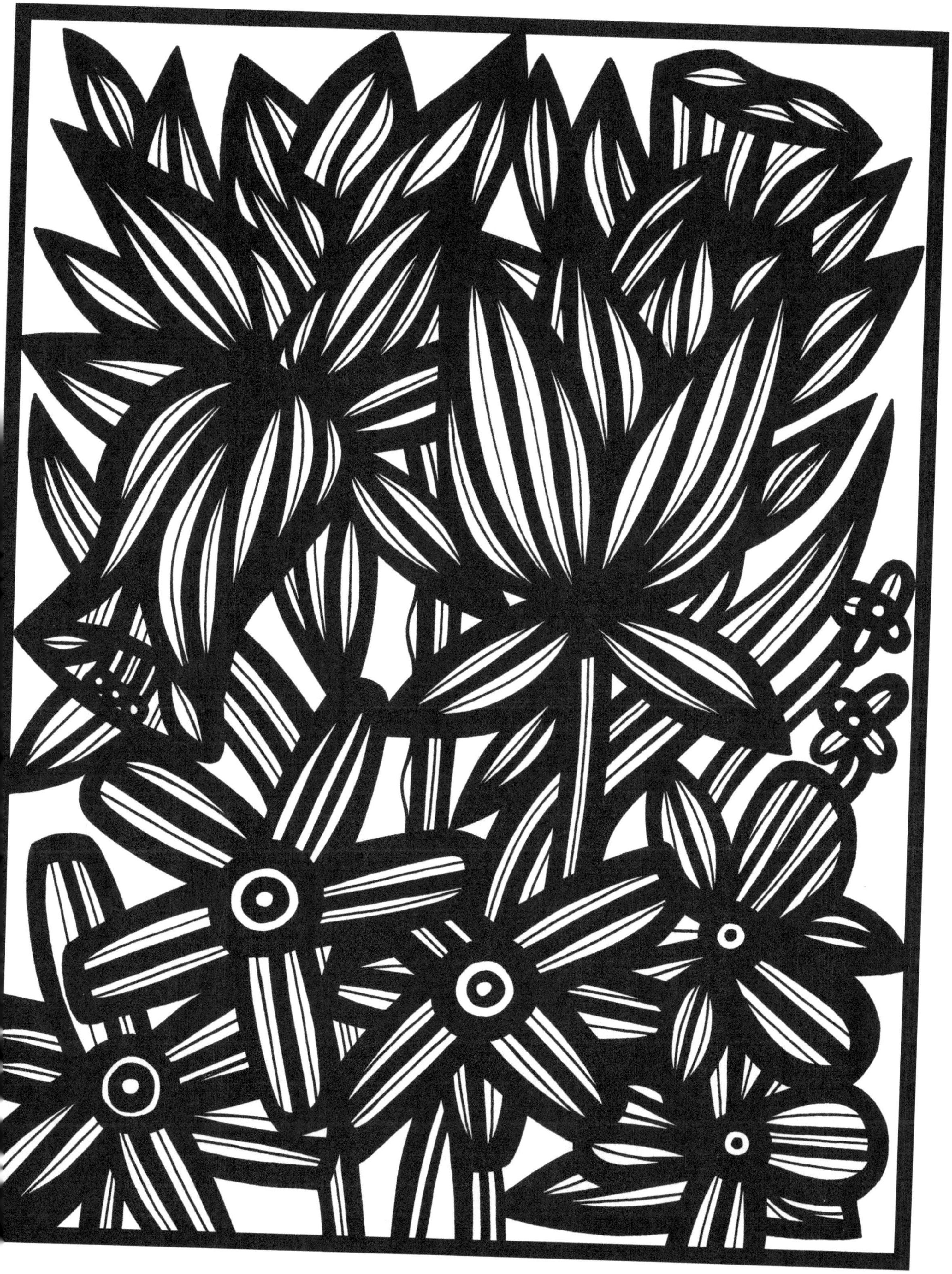

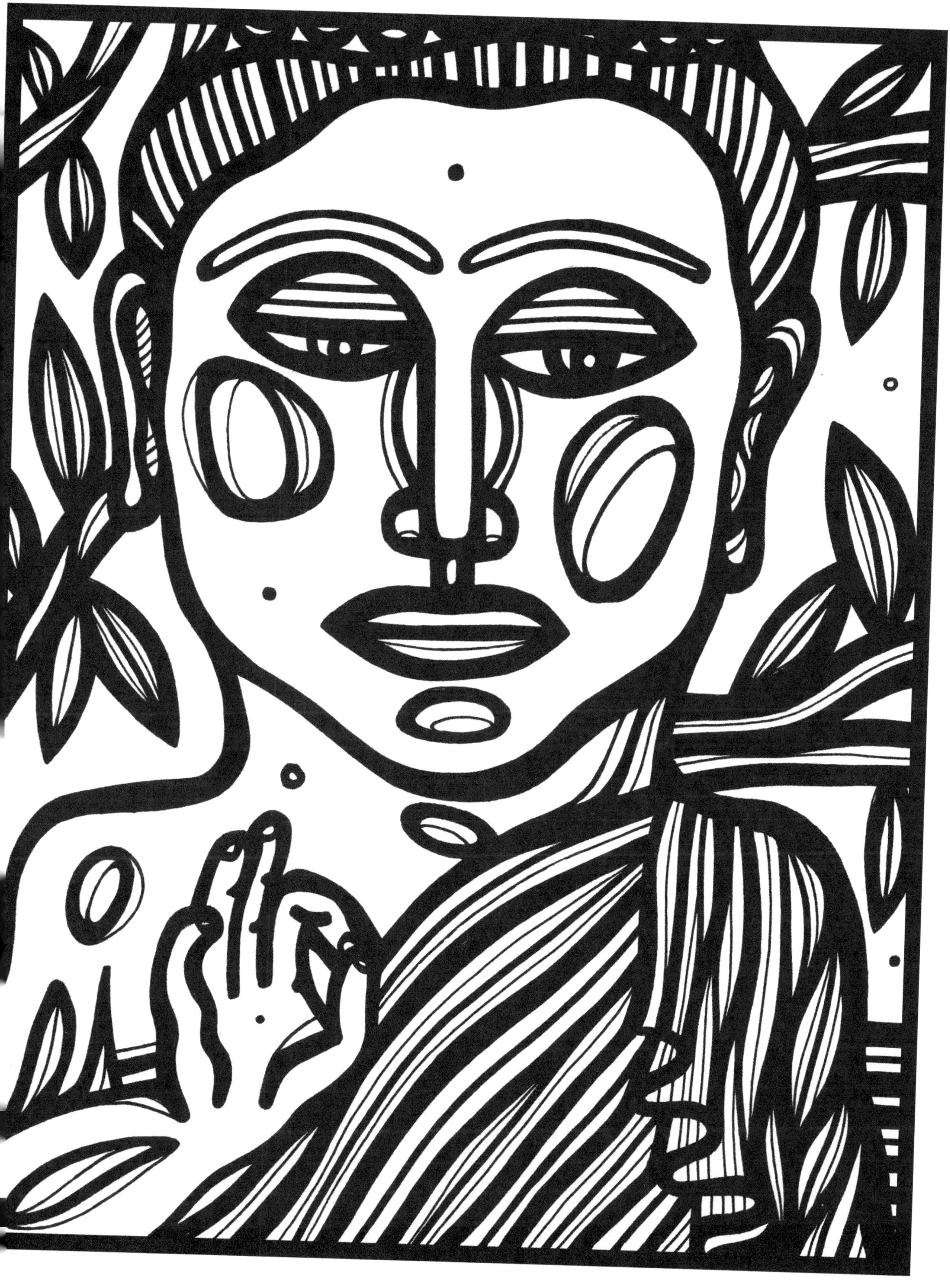

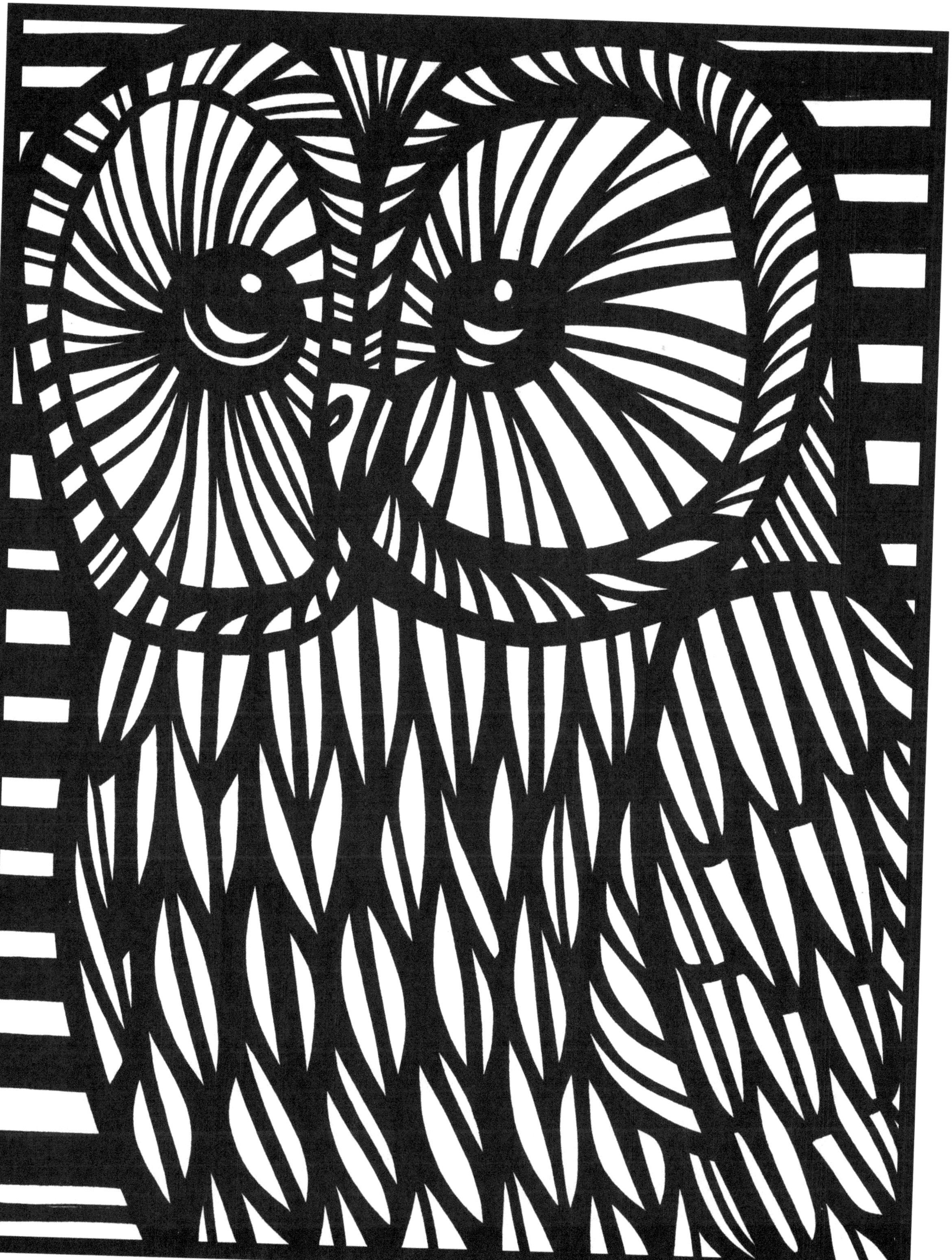

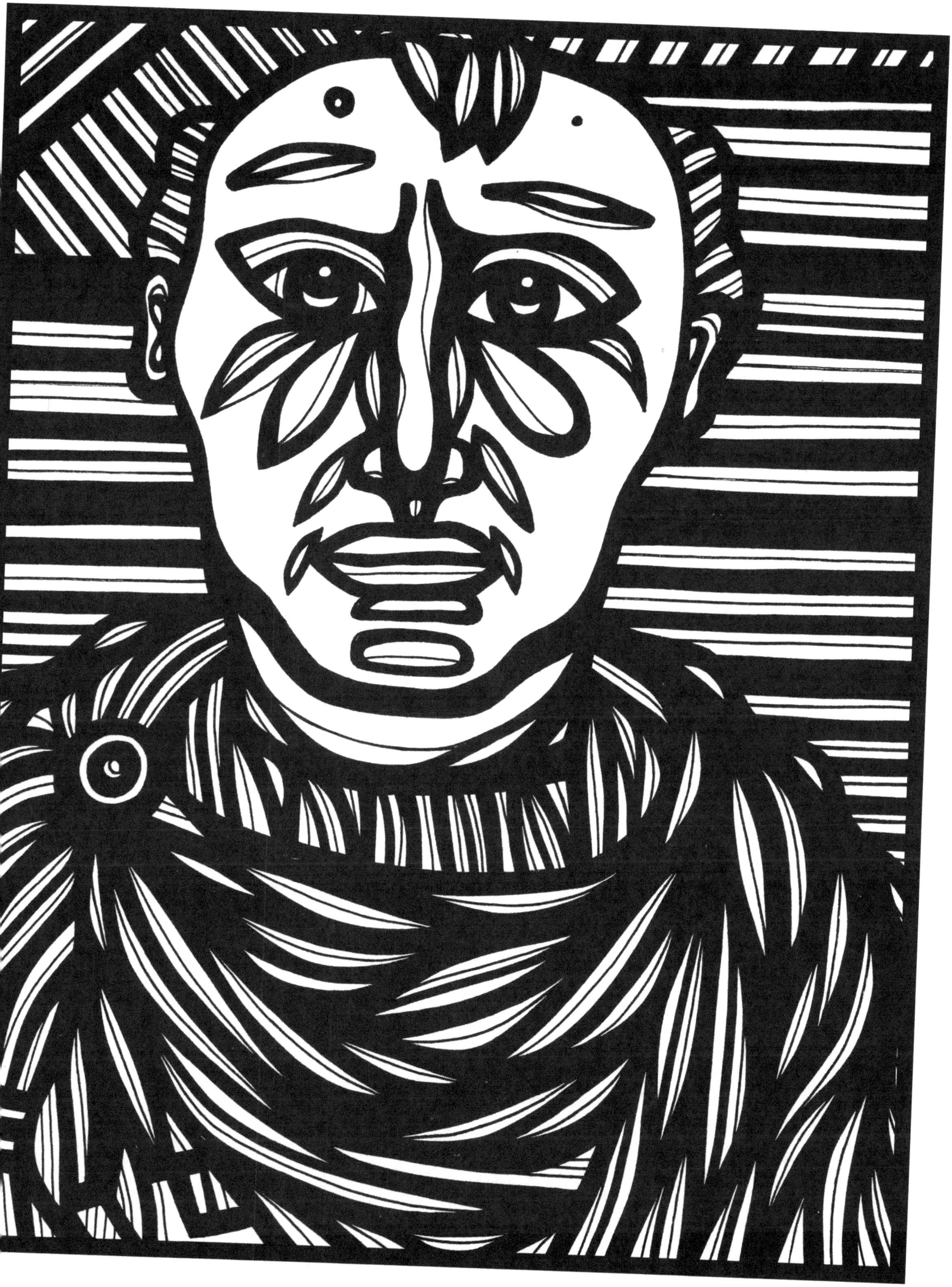

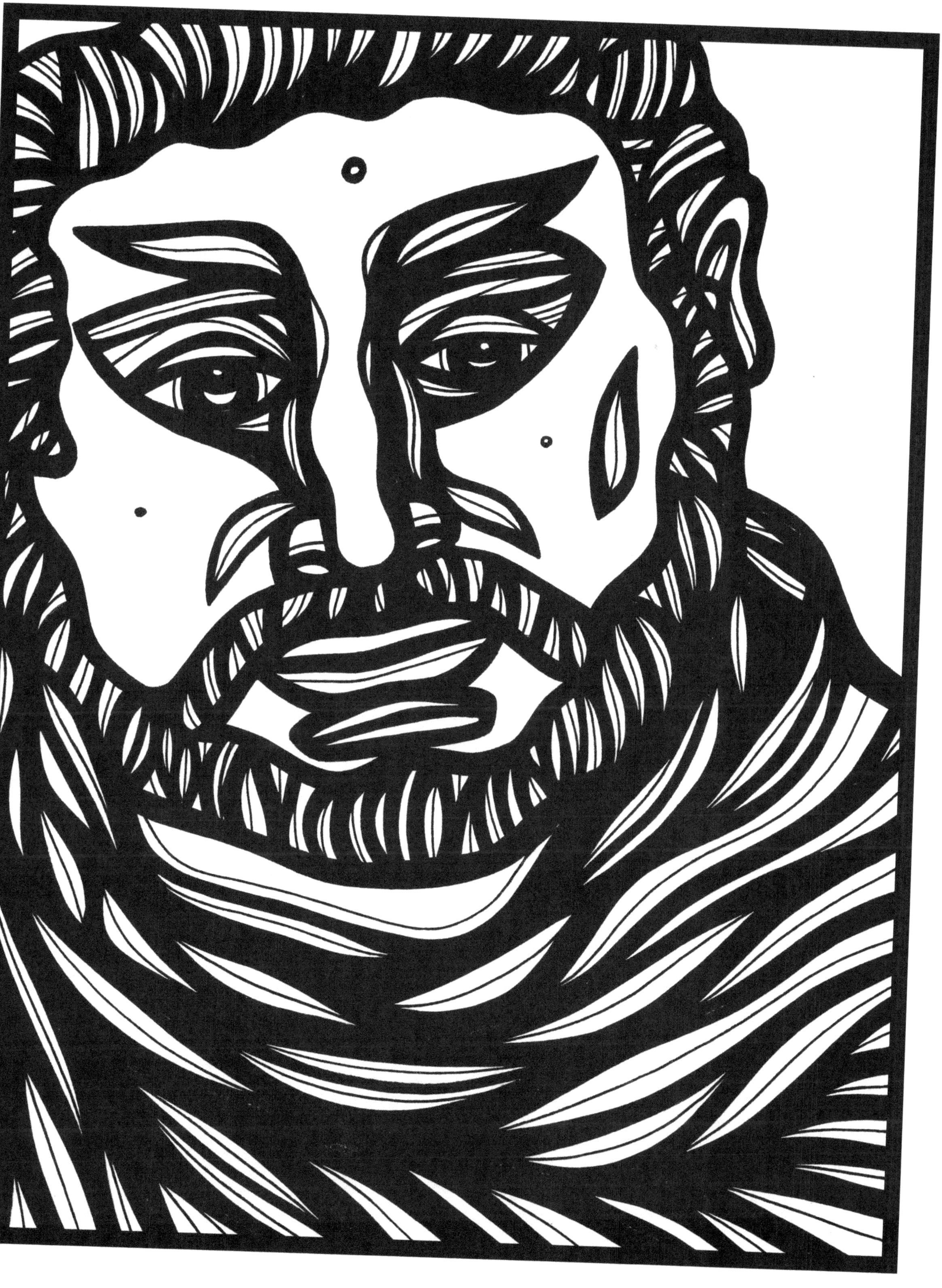

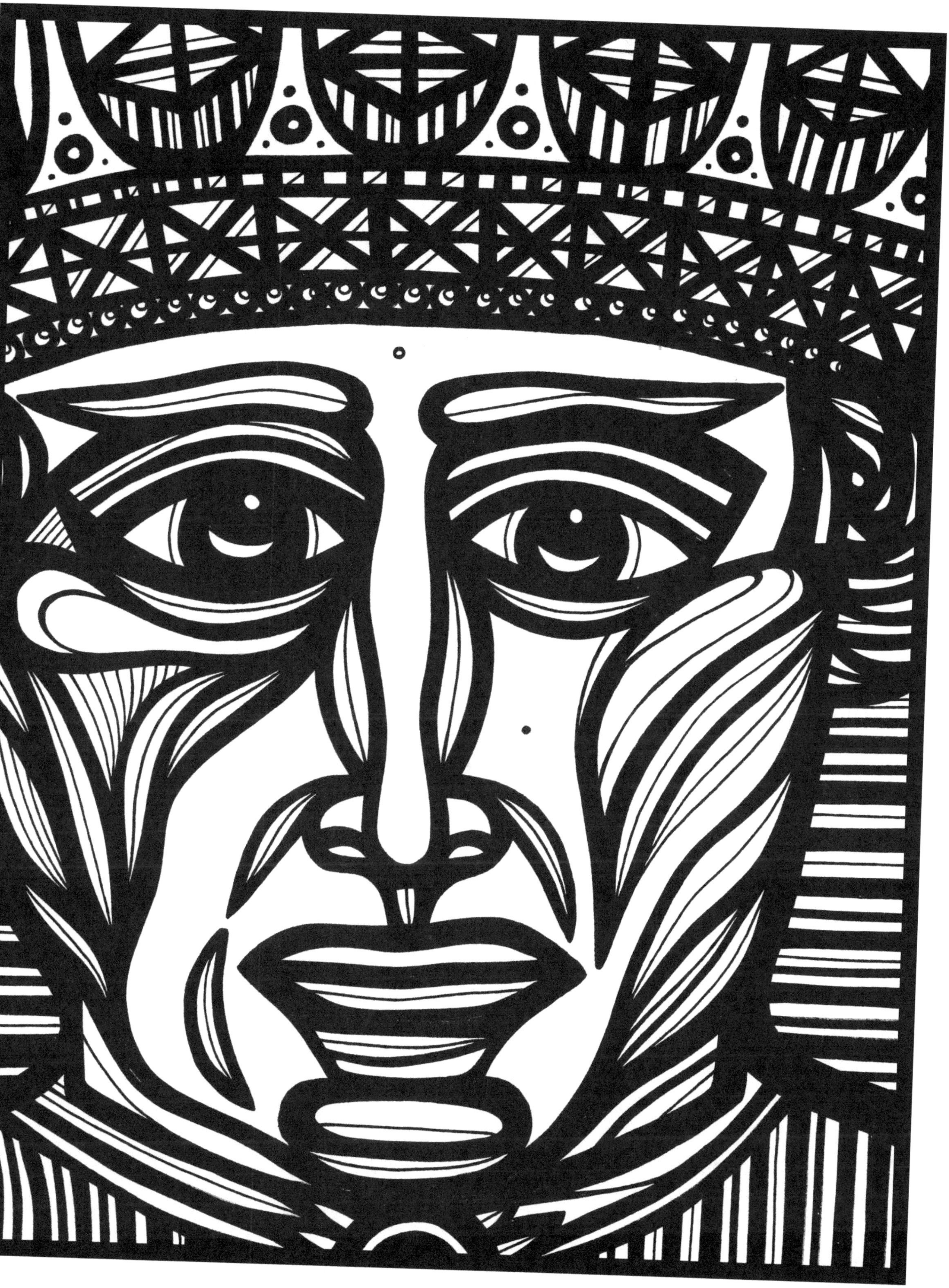

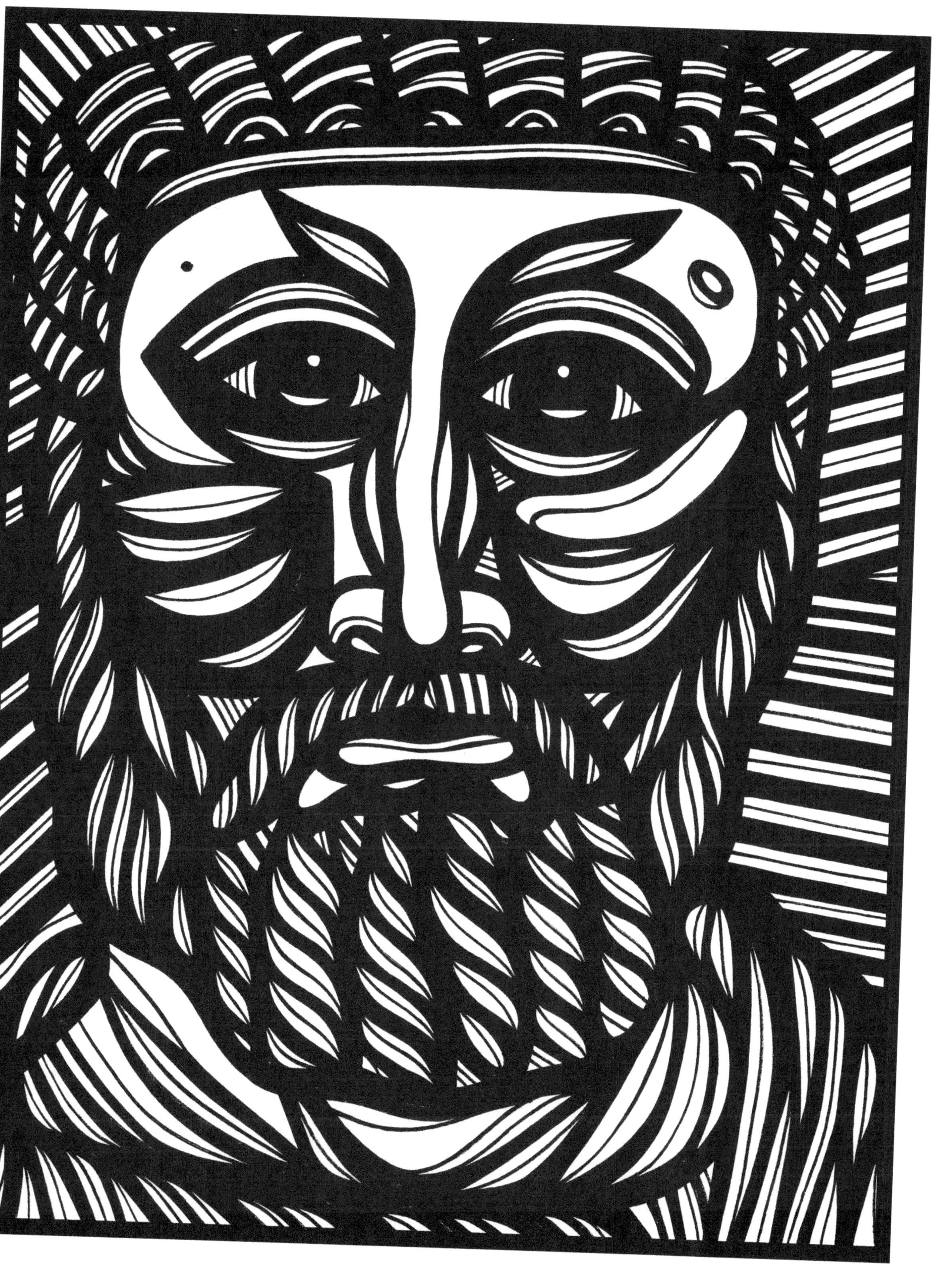

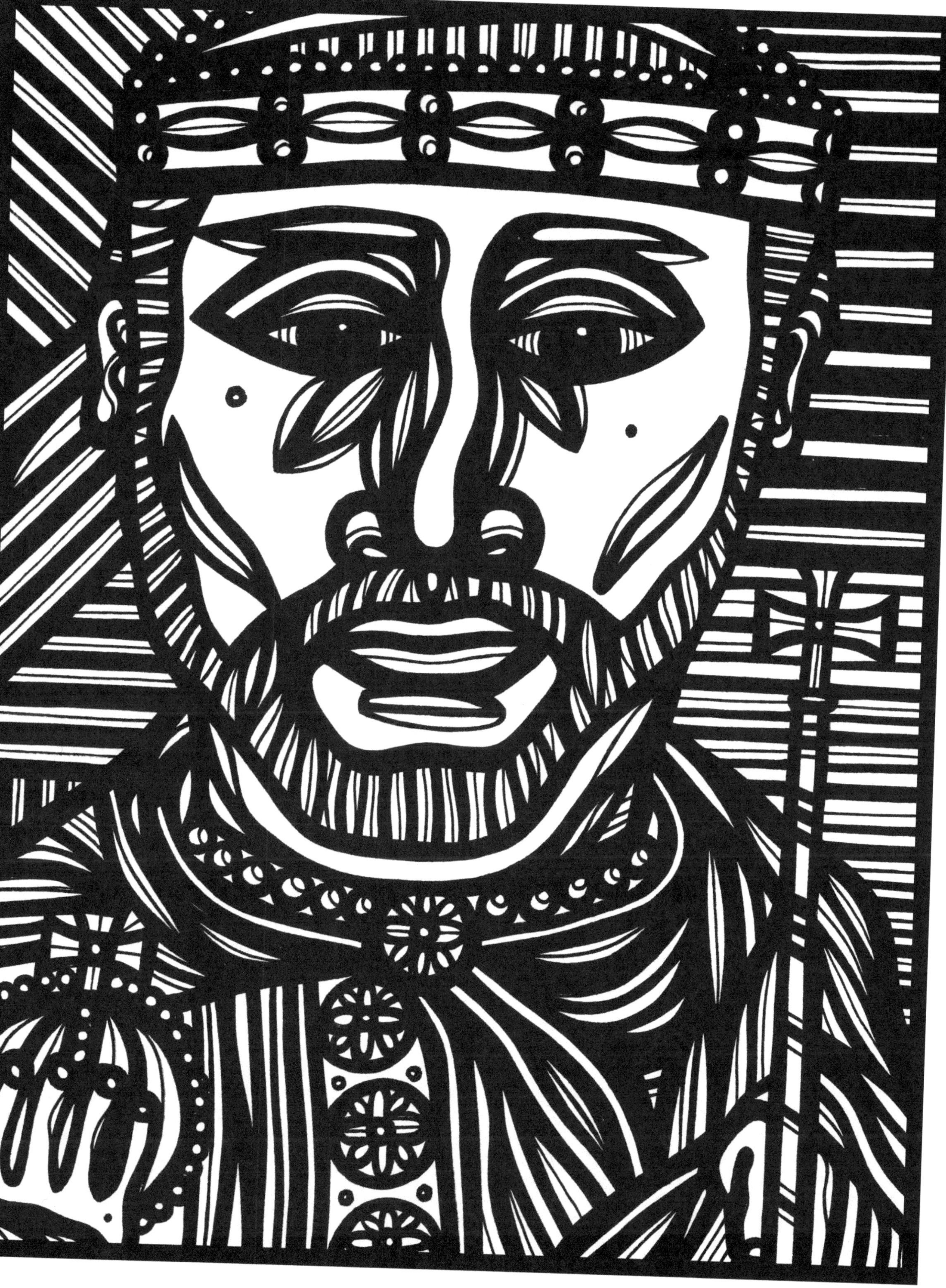

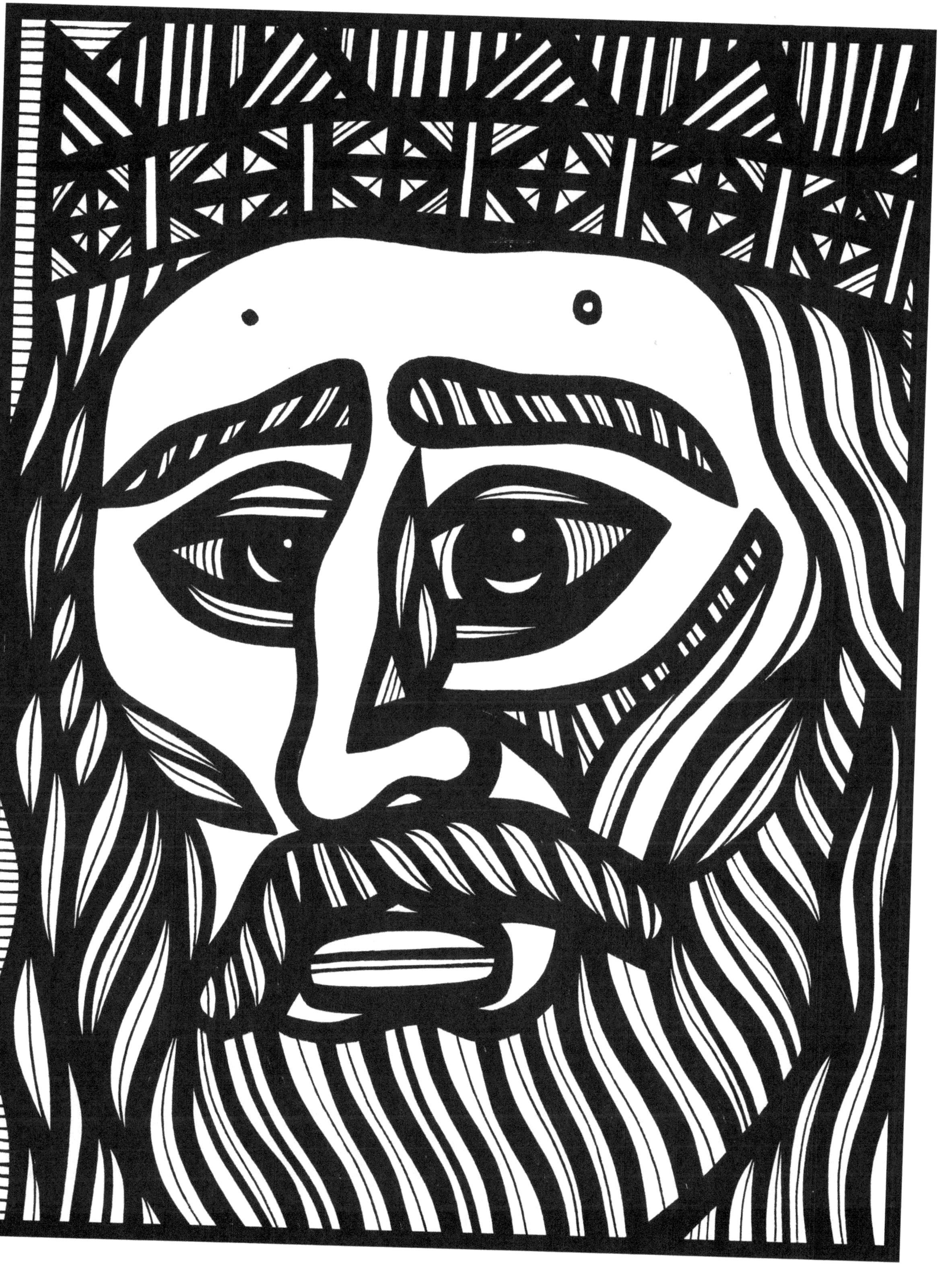

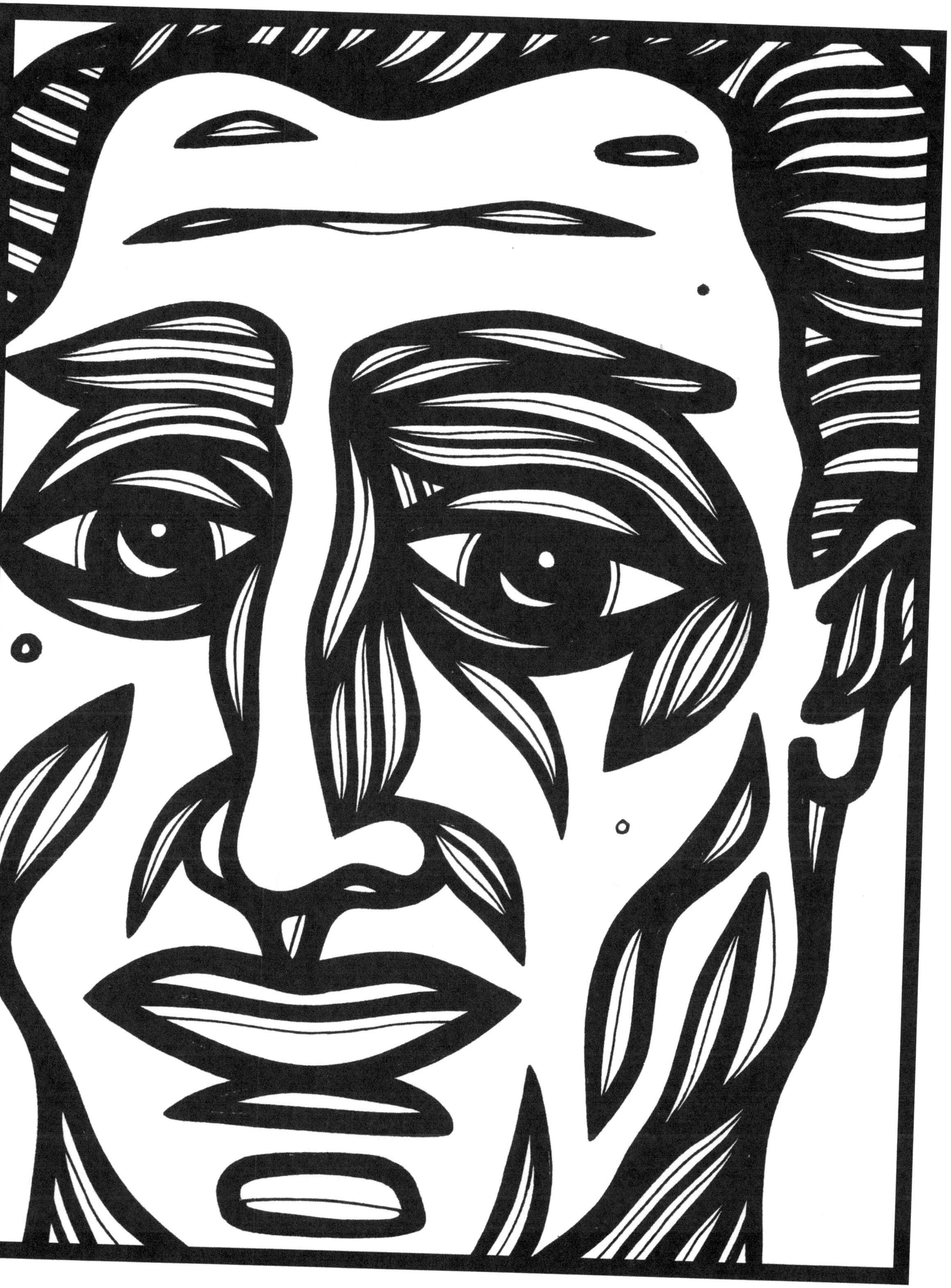

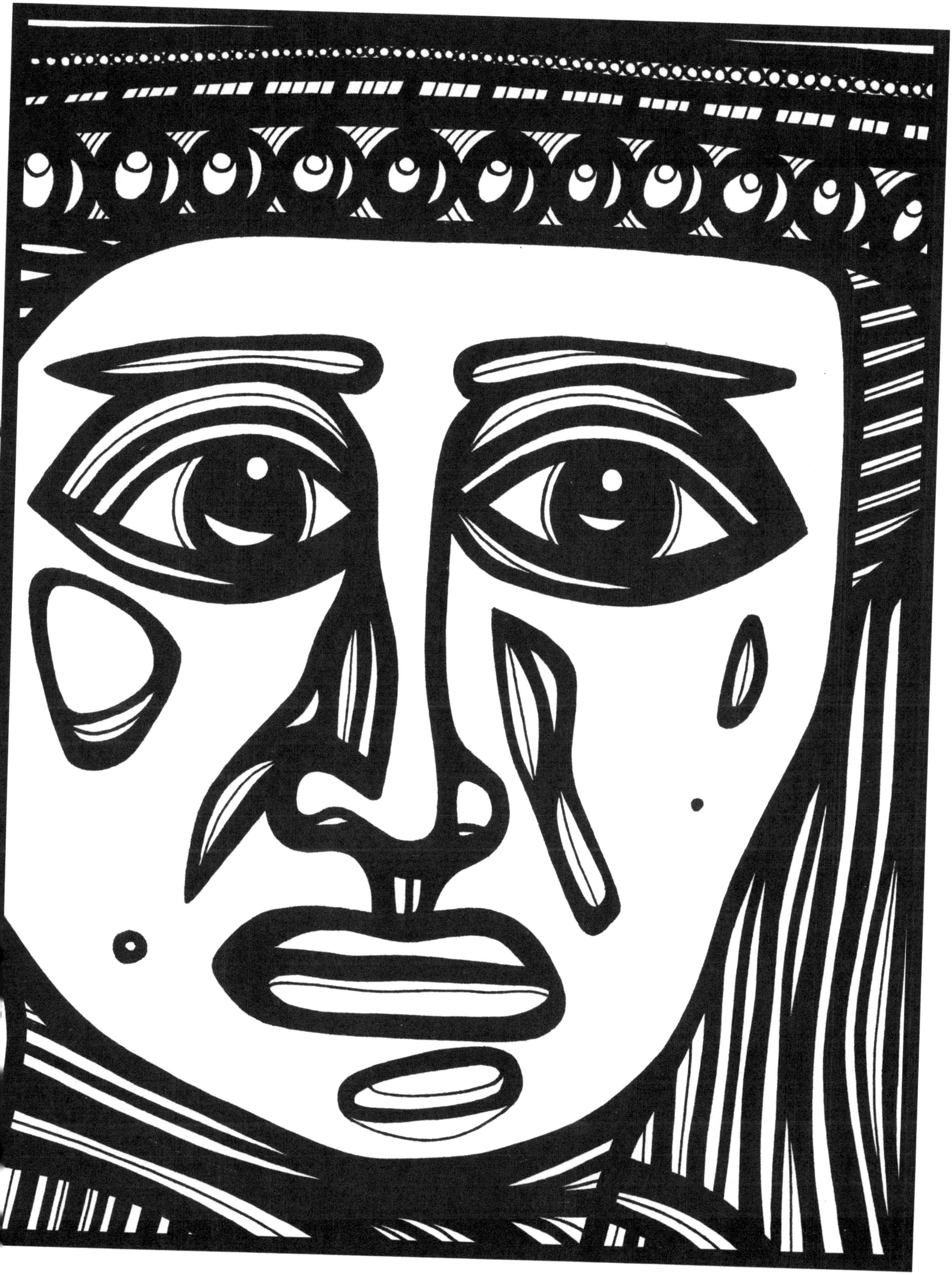

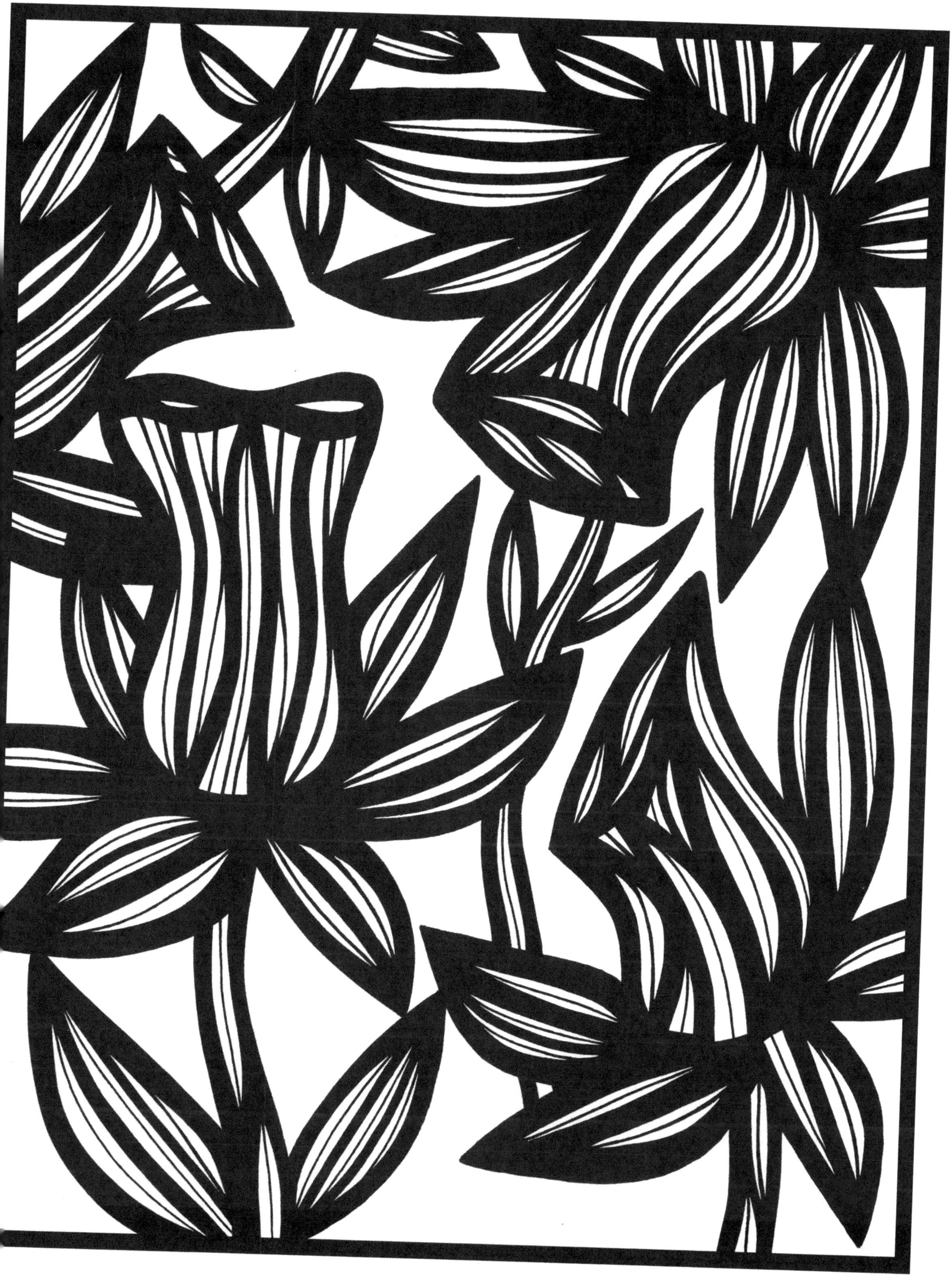

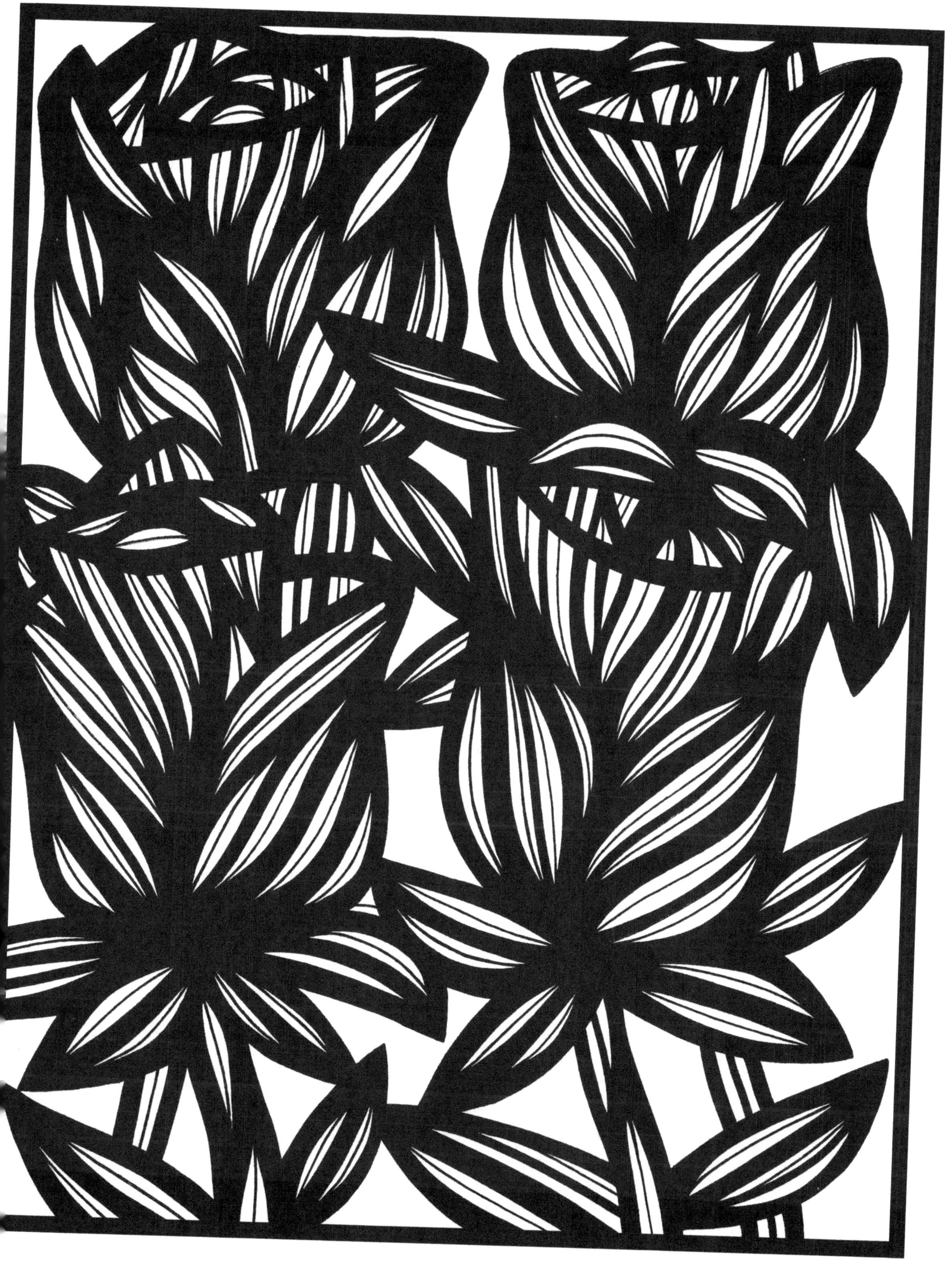

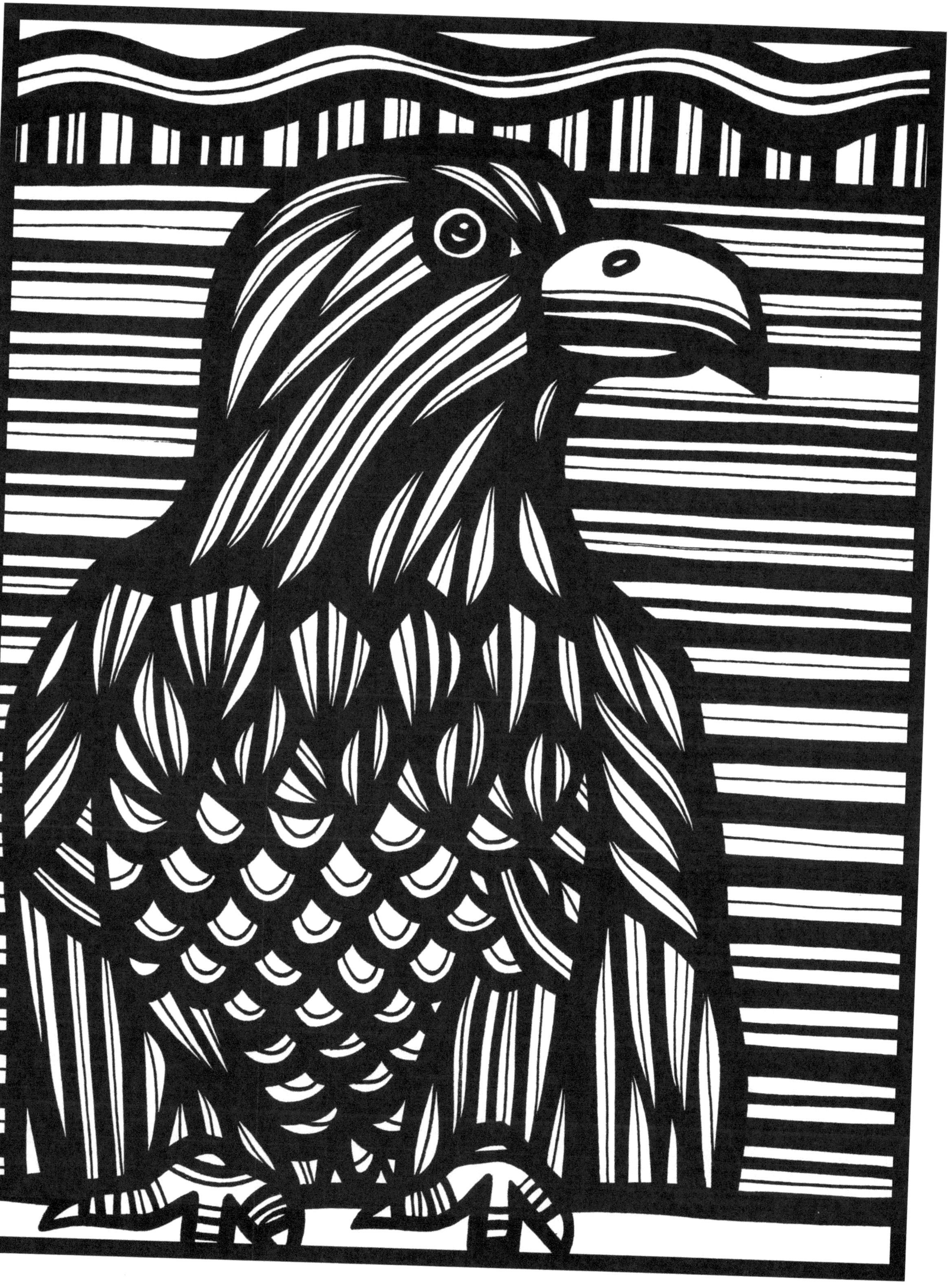

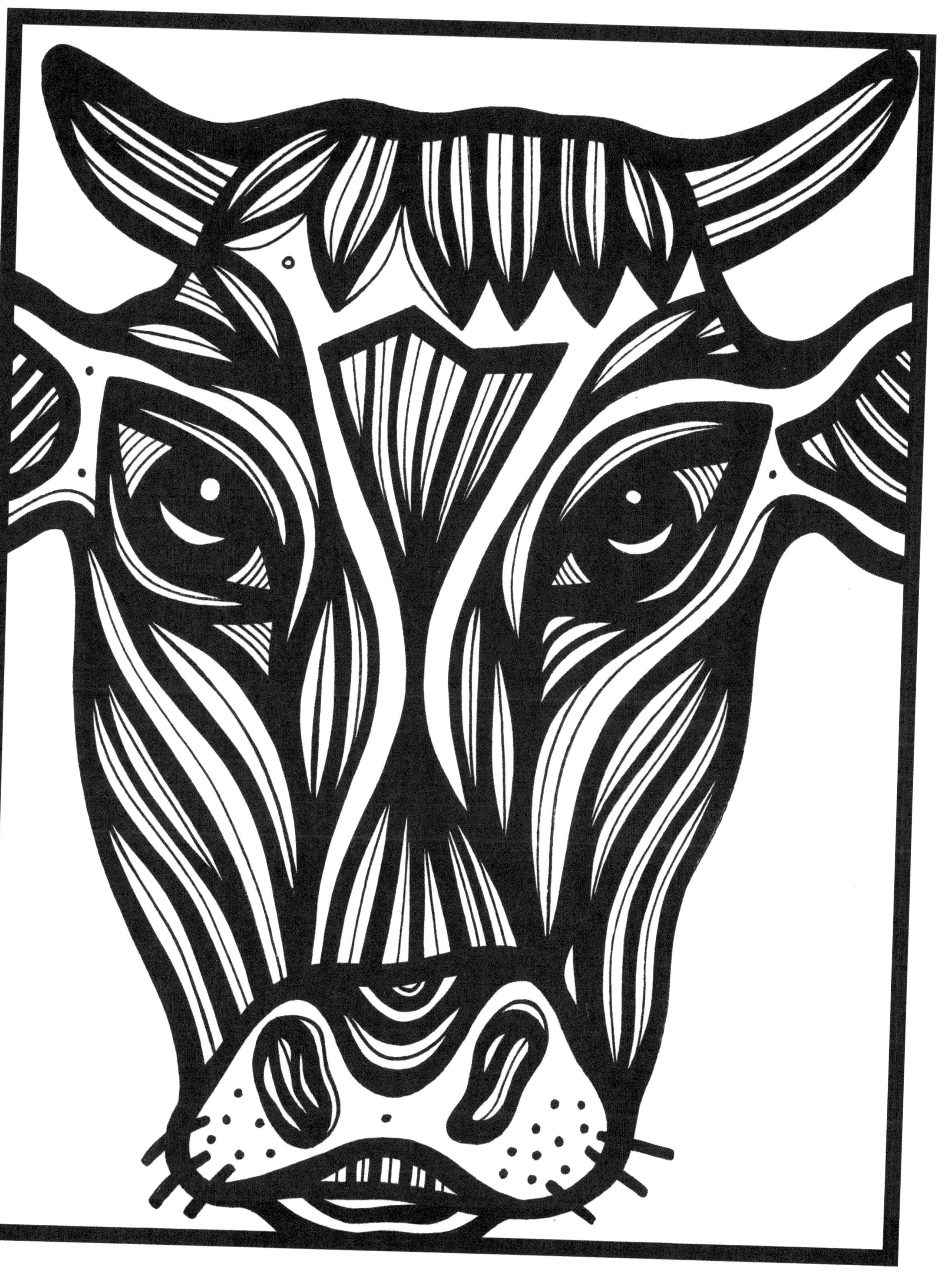

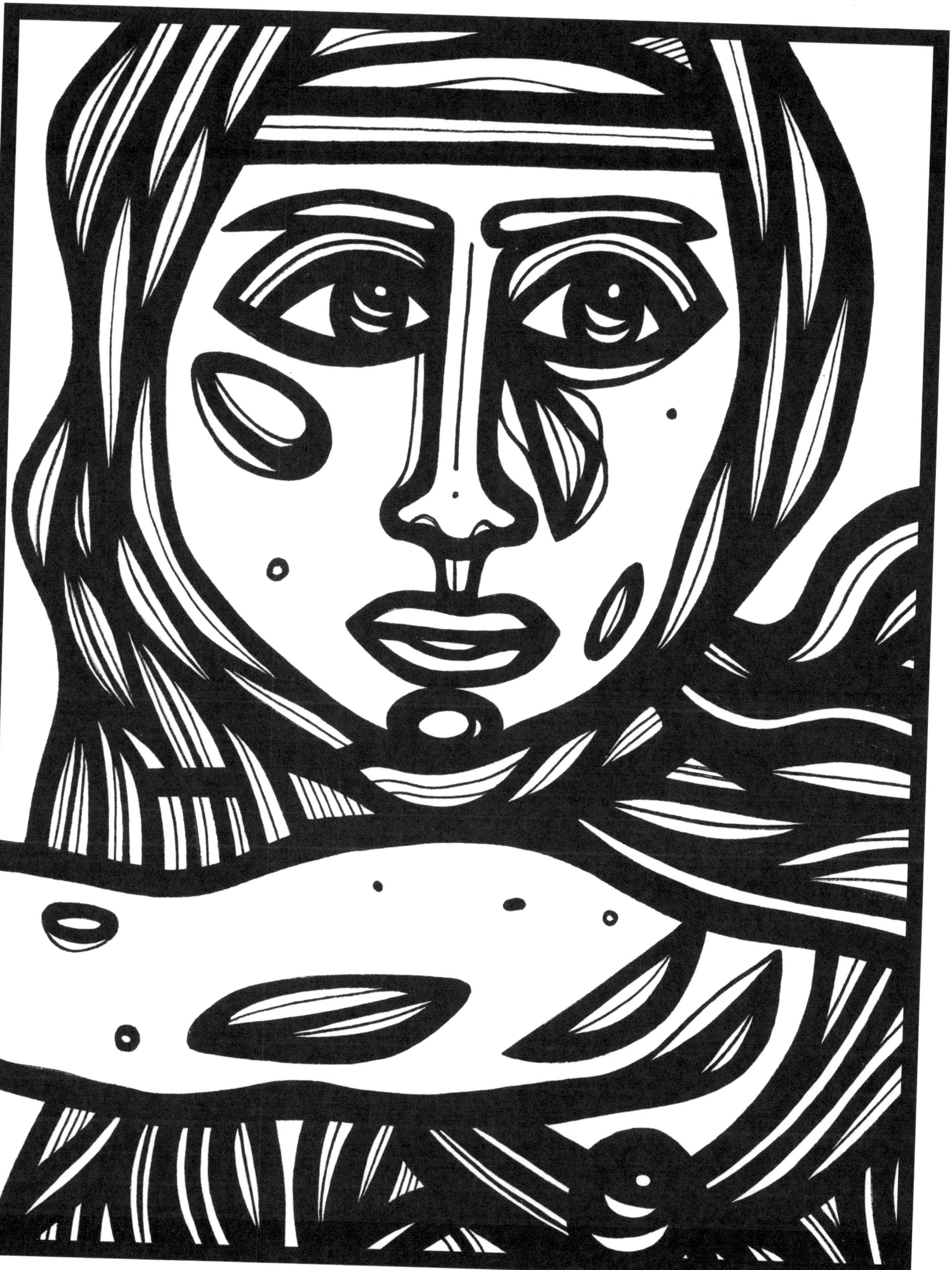

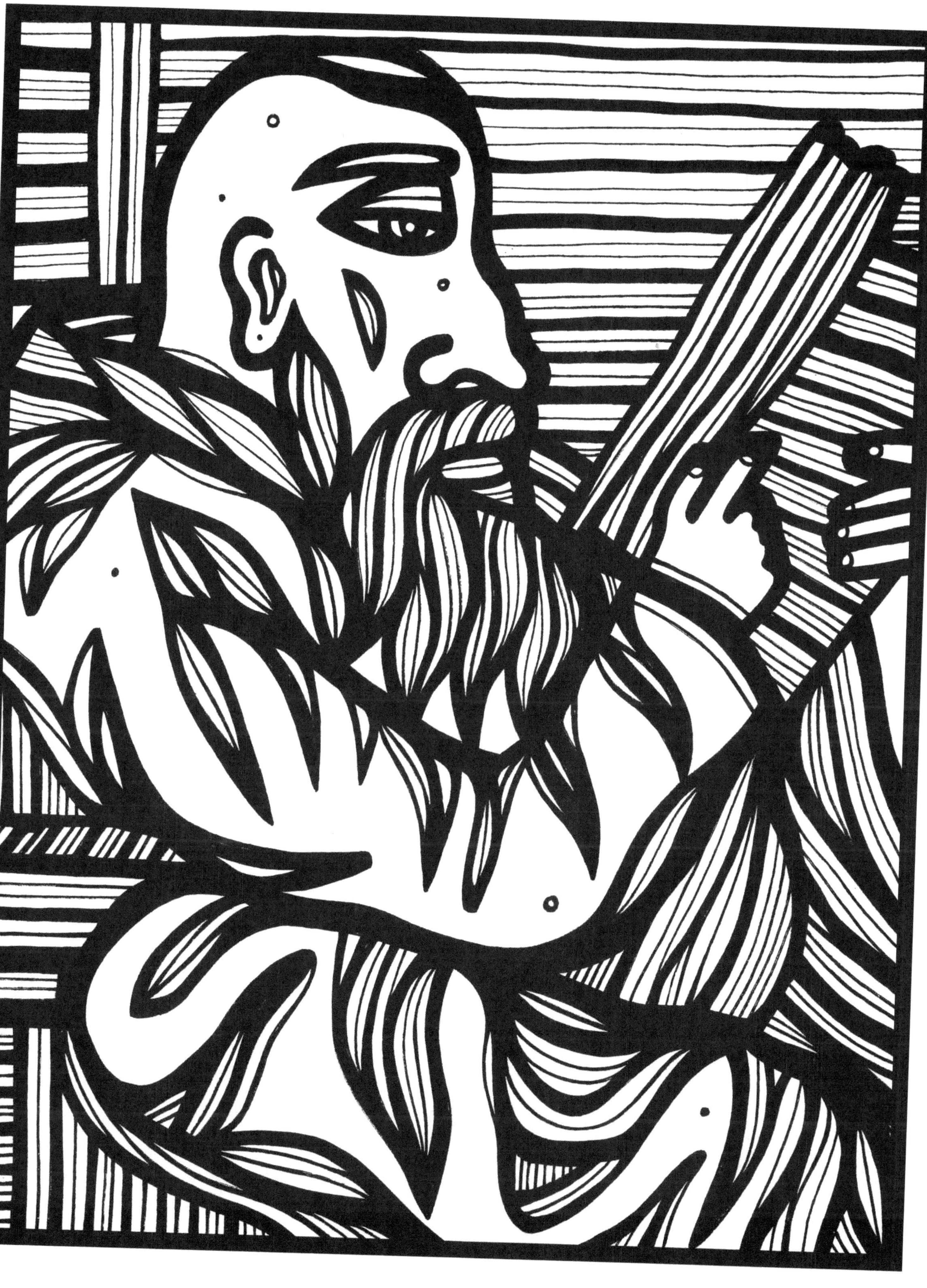

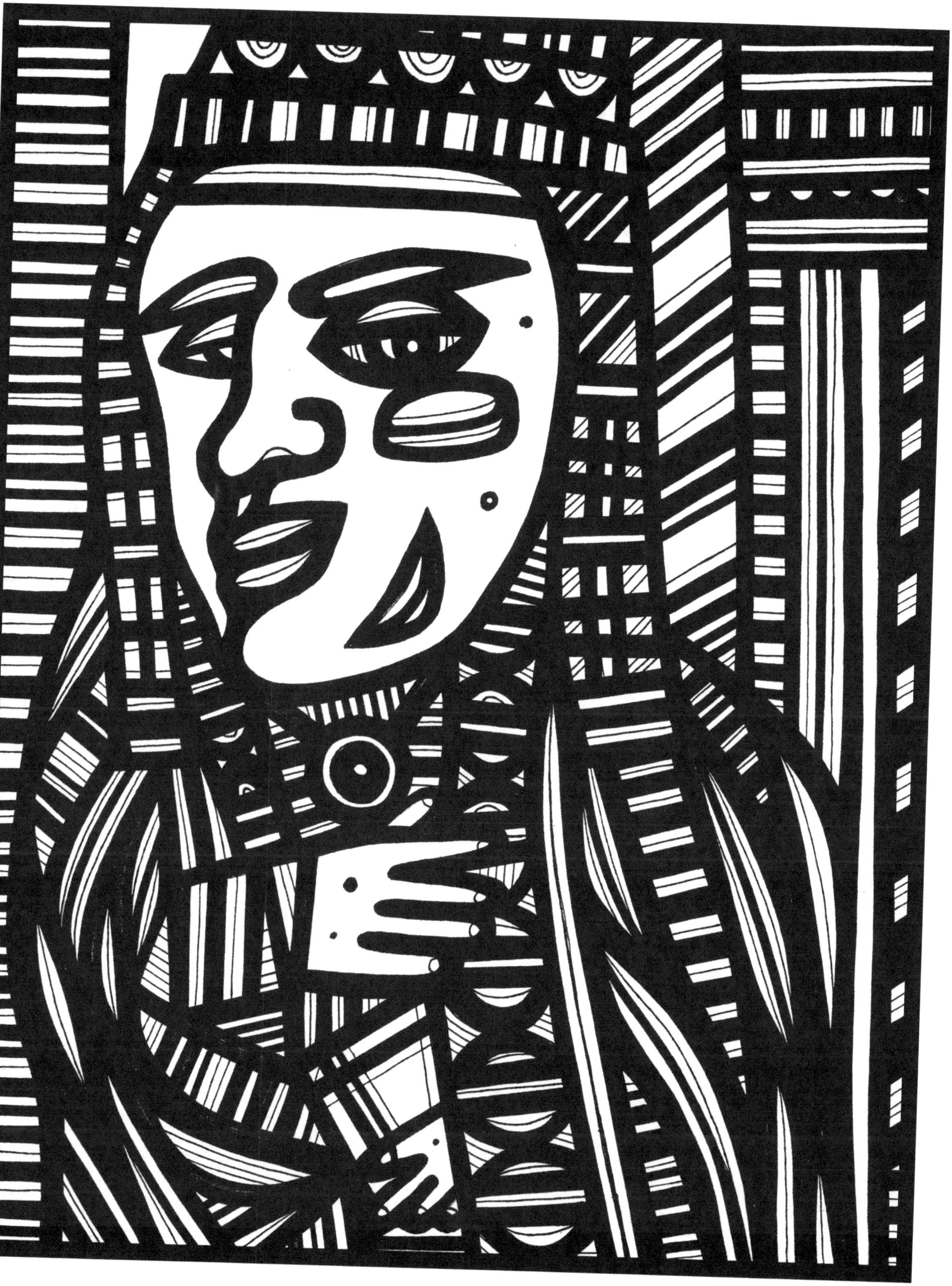

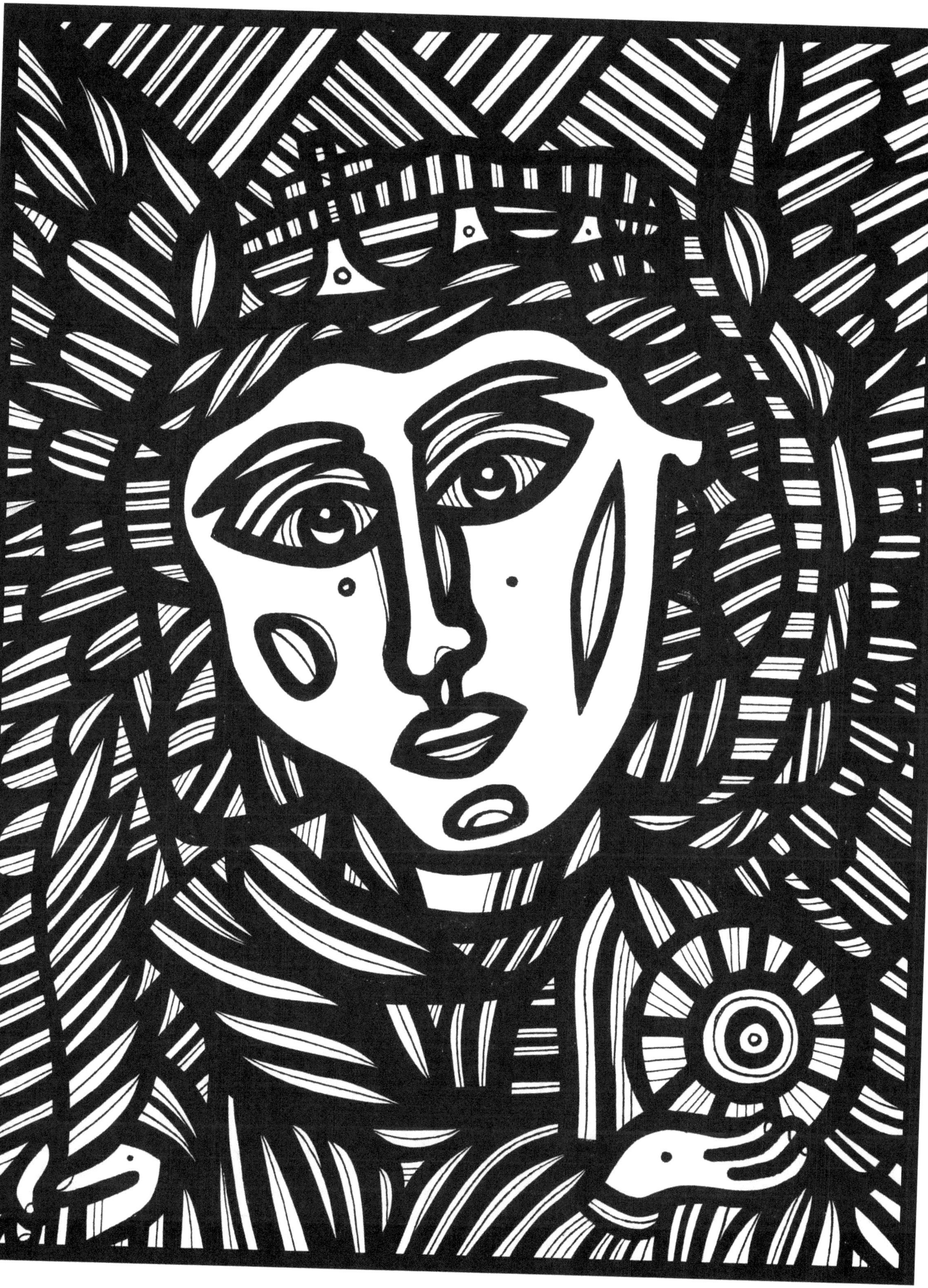

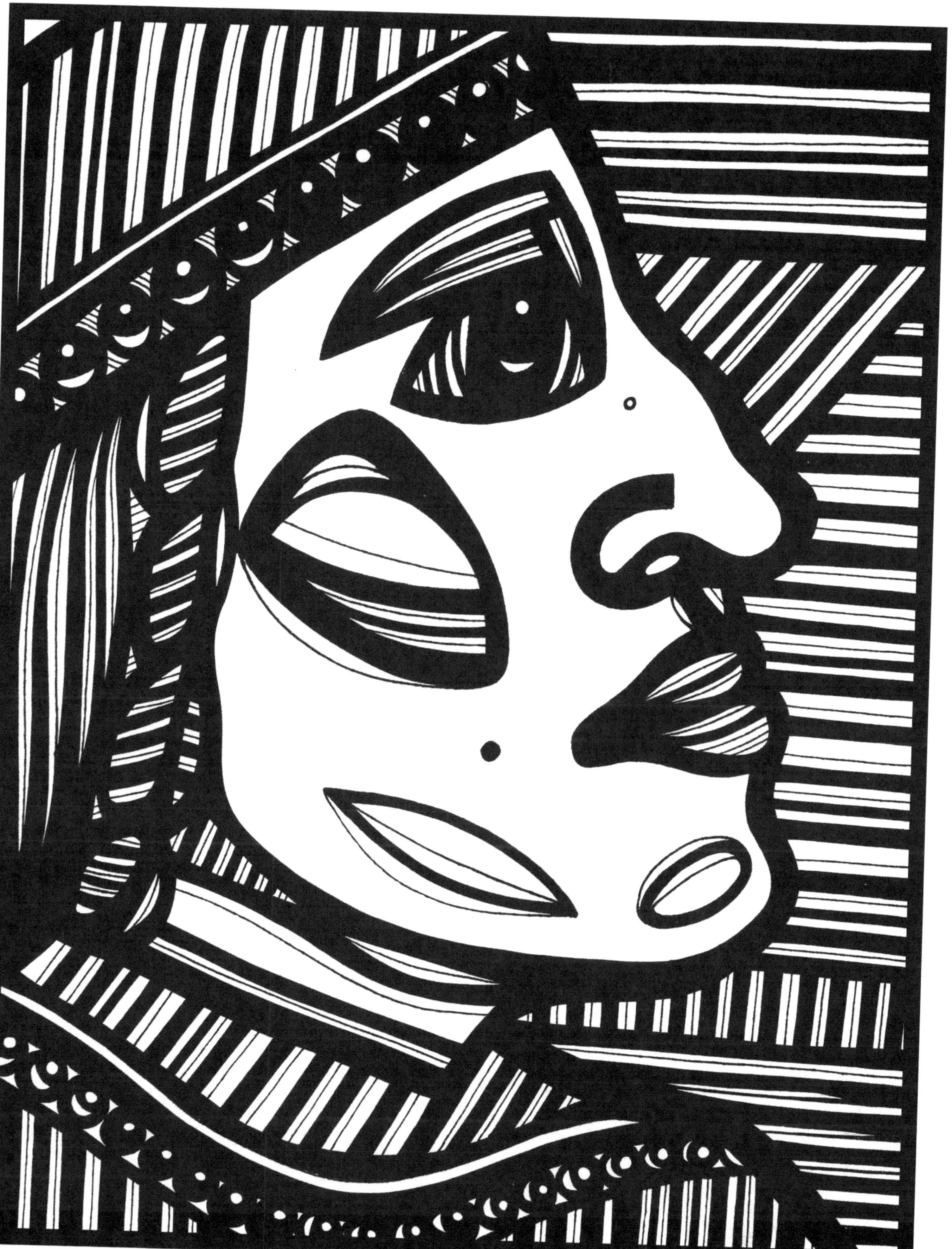

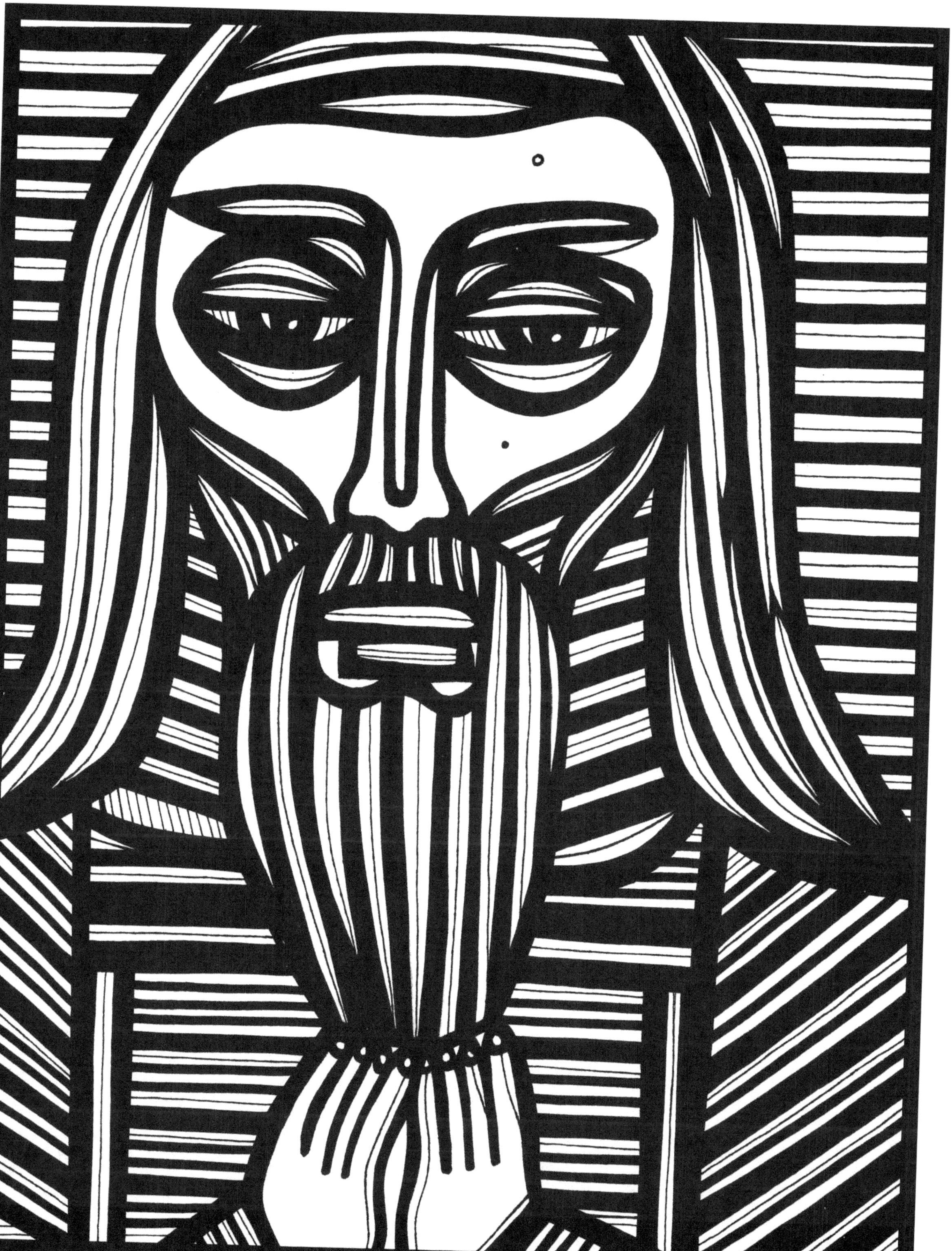

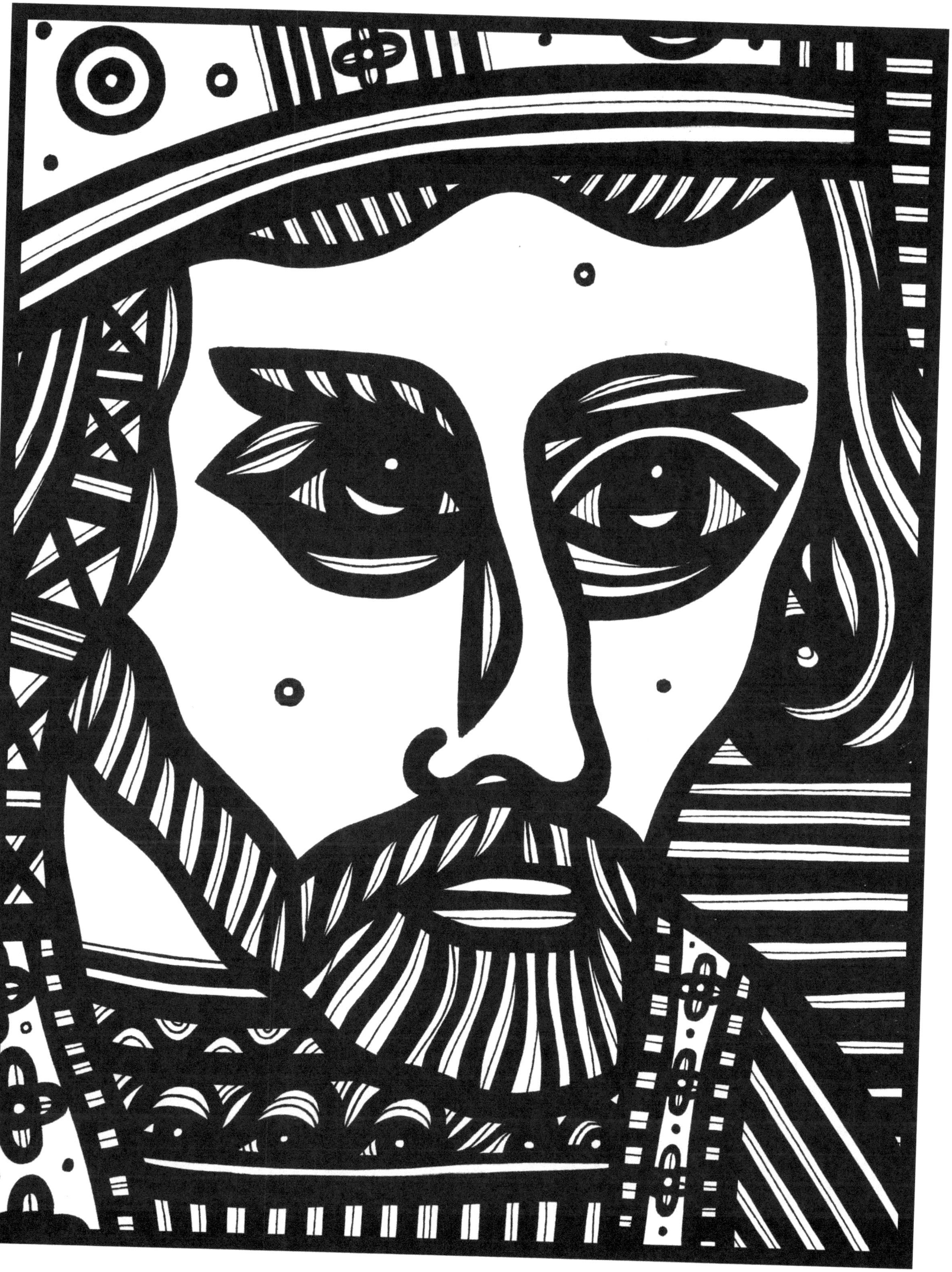

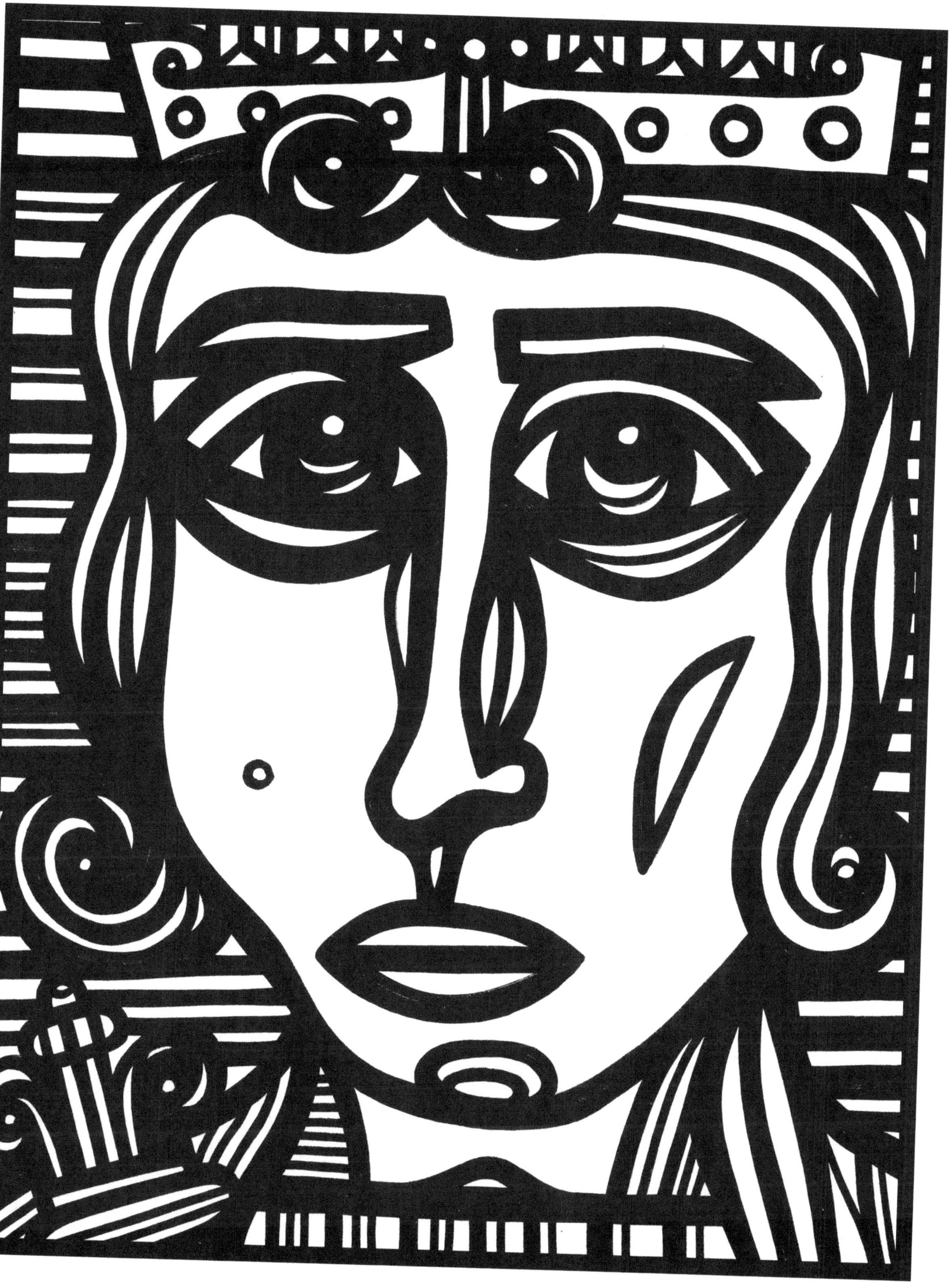

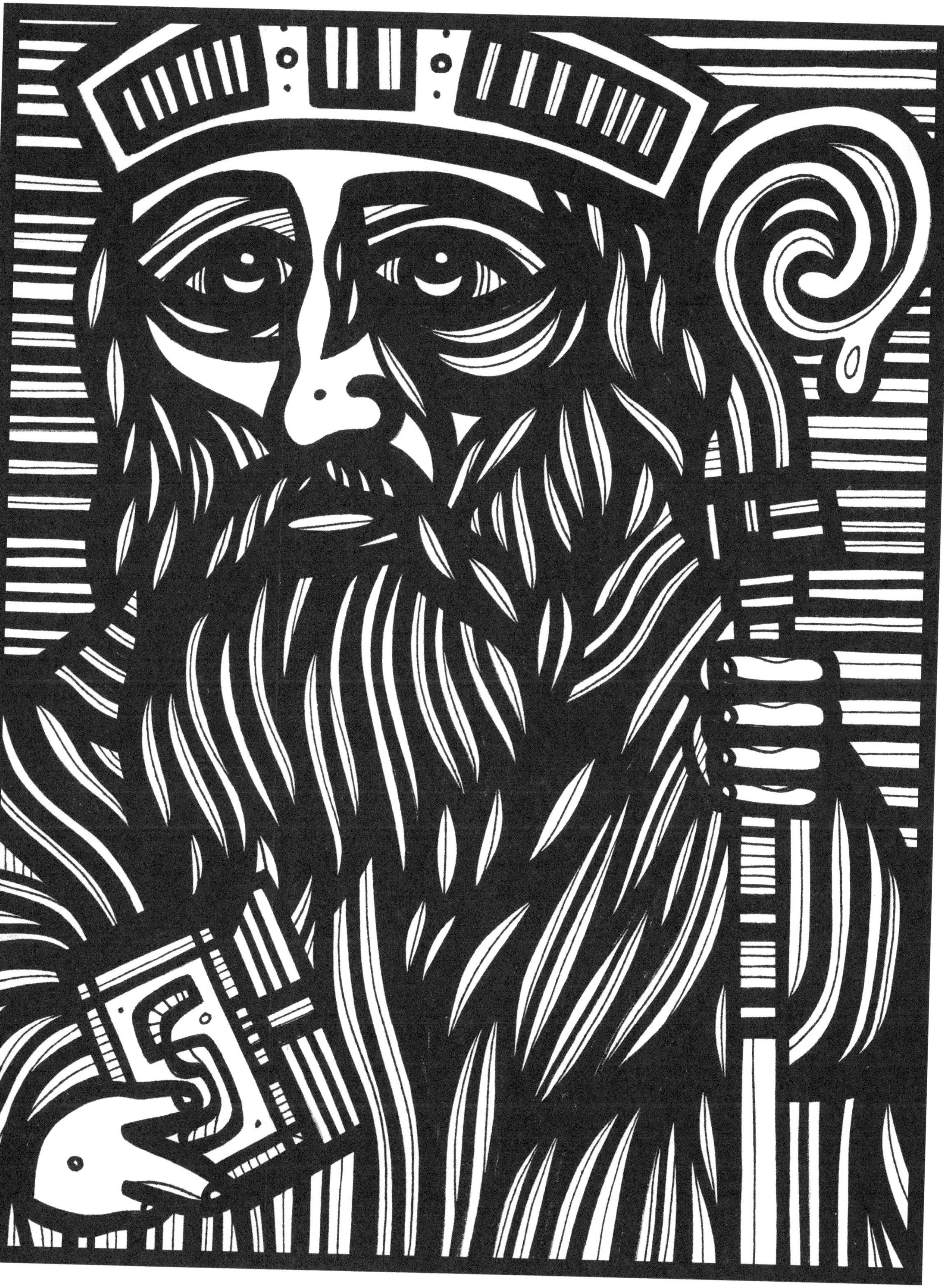

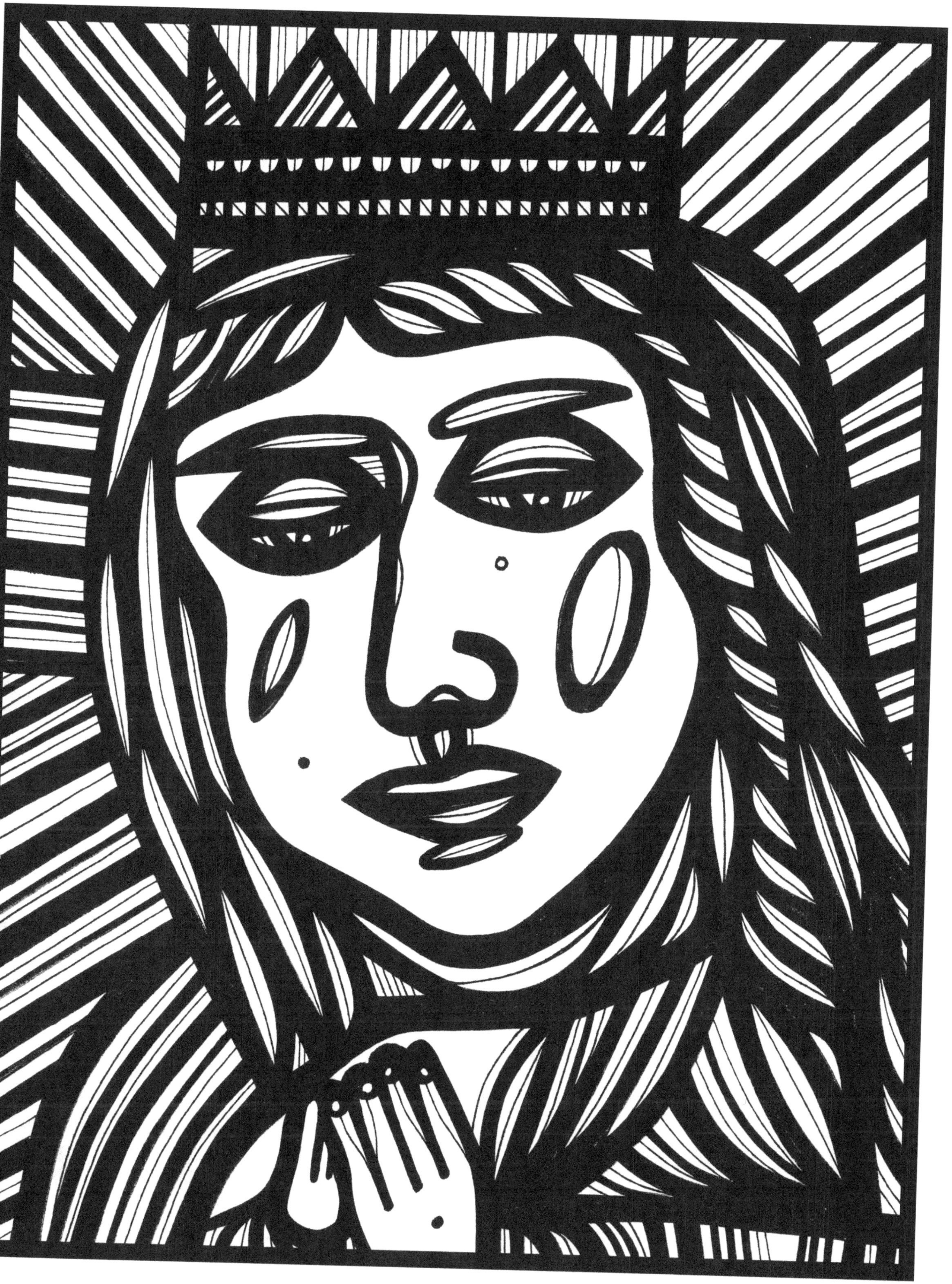

THE END,
THANK YOU.
COPYRIGHT 2020
BY EDDIE ALFARO
ALL RIGHTS RESERVED.
MORE BOOKS:
631ART.COM

www.ingramcontent.com/pod-product-compliance
Lightning Source LLC
Chambersburg PA
CBHW080136240526
45468CB00009BA/2464
9781795623476